D0266466

Thankyou for buying our annual
Thankyou for watching us on the telly
Thankyou for listening to our records
Thankyou for coming to see us on tour
thankyou for everything you have done to help us
carry on having a laugh.
       Love, Jason
       xxx

P.S. Thankyou

No words I can write can thankyou all enough.
for the year you have just given us, you've helped us
once again to really enjoy ourselves and we hope we
have given you just as much fun, please always stay
as happy as can be and heres to another great year
       God bless and keep smiling
       Your bestest mate
       Mark!

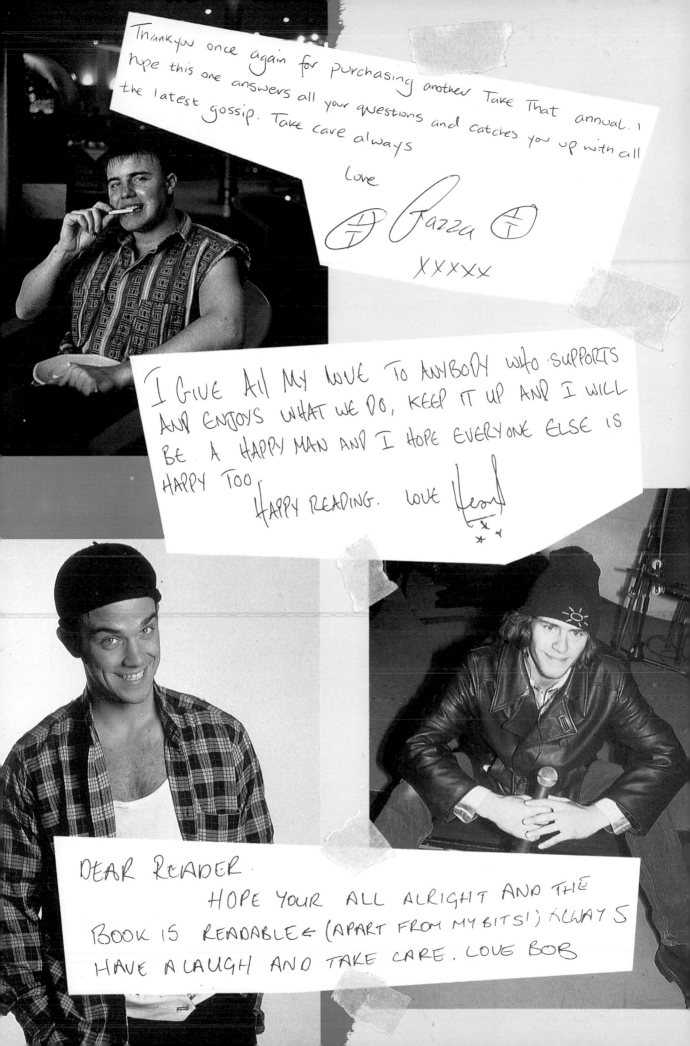

Thankyou once again for purchasing another Take That annual. I hope this one answers all your questions and catches you up with all the latest gossip. Take care always

Love

Gazza

XXXXX

I GIVE ALL MY LOVE TO ANYBODY WHO SUPPORTS AND ENJOYS WHAT WE DO, KEEP IT UP AND I WILL BE A HAPPY MAN AND I HOPE EVERYONE ELSE IS HAPPY TOO. HAPPY READING. LOVE Howard
x x

DEAR READER,
HOPE YOUR ALL ALRIGHT AND THE BOOK IS READABLE (APART FROM MY BITS!) ALWAYS HAVE A LAUGH AND TAKE CARE. LOVE BOB

CONTENTS

© 1994 Take That
Under licence from Nice Man Merchandising.

Written by Michael Heatley.
Edited by Melanie J Clayden.
Design by Louise Ivimy.
Photography by Philip Ollerenshaw/Idols.

Published by
GRANDREAMS LIMITED
Jadwin House, 205/211 Kentish Town Road,
London, NW5 2JU.

Printed in Italy.

"All I really ever wanted was a record deal" Gary

No doubt about it, Gary Barlow is a born musician. Growing up in Frodsham, Cheshire, his mother Marjorie was a science technician at the local high school, which meant he really had to toe the line in the classroom! Marjorie would have liked her son to become a policeman or work in a bank, but Gary's early interest in music was obvious.

A big Adam Ant fan, his first musical venture was a school band based on *Adam and the Ants*. They reproduced the twin drum sound by bashing away at biscuit tins! Gary also took the lead role in a school production of *Joseph And The Amazing Technicolor Dreamcoat* when he was ten. "From an early age, I was a real entertainer," he recalls. "I'd do impressions of my neighbours, my friends and especially the teachers."

It was his mother who encouraged him to take part in a labour club talent contest at the age of ten and even taught him a few jokes to incorporate into his stage routine! Gary came second with his rendition of 'A Whiter Shade Of Pale', and his performance won him a Saturday night residency at the club.

Then, when he was eleven, his parents asked him whether he wanted a keyboard or a BMX bike for Christmas - for Gary, there was no contest! However, within months, he'd exhausted the keyboard's possibilities and was ready to move on to something more complex. Recognising his son's talent, Gary's father Colin splashed out £600 to buy him an organ. "It was enormous, it virtually filled my bedroom," Gary laughs. "I started playing straight away and within about six months, I was really good."

He started to find work as a freelance organist and at the age of thirteen, formed a duo with a girl from school called Heather. His schoolwork was left behind as Gary became more and more interested in a musical career. By the time he was fourteen, he was backing showbiz stars like Ken Dodd and earning £140 a week!

However, Gary's big break came when his music teacher, Mrs Nelson, encouraged him to enter Pebble Mill's 'A Song For Christmas' competition. He submitted a song called 'Let's Pray For Christmas', which was short-listed and recorded for the programme, winning the semi-final but not the final. Nevertheless, the competition gave him recording experience and helped him to make contacts encouraging his songwriting.

The formation of *Take That* was first suggested to Gary when he met Nigel Martin Smith, the band's present manager. Armed with songs of the calibre of 'Another Crack In My Heart' and 'A Million Love Songs', which were written when Gary was still only sixteen, *Take That* simply couldn't fail.

As soon as he earned some money from the band, Gary invested it in a three bedroom bungalow in the Cheshire countryside with a studio built onto the back. Gary works there every day when he is not on the road and his songwriting skills continue to grow from strength to strength.

"All I really ever wanted was a record deal and to be famous," he says simply. And at the age of twenty-three, he's succeeded on both counts.

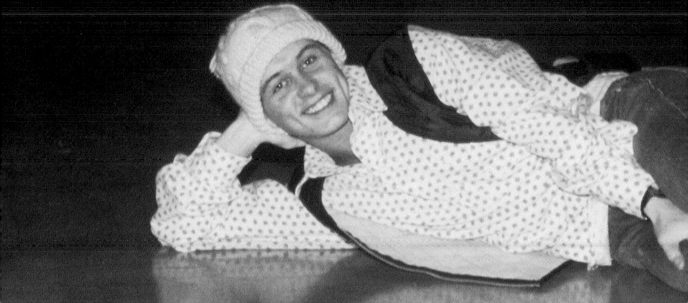

My Manchester

Take That spend so much time away from home that when they do get some time off, there's no better way of spending it than relaxing in Manchester amongst family and friends.

Ask *Take That* what's so special about Manchester, and they'll unanimously reply that it's the warmth of its people that makes you feel at home. "The people in and around Manchester are all very friendly," says Mark. "It always rains so there's no worry of drought(!), and all my family and friends live there!"

According to *Take That*, Manchester's great attractions include Aflecks Palace, a three storey building of second-hand delights where Mark and Jason can often be seen and Zuttis, where Mark used to work on leaving school and where he often pops back on a visit. Jason's 'personal highlights tour' also includes Albert Square, Brahms & Lizst (the bar that is) and "my mum - top lady!" As far as *Take That* are concerned, it isn't worth making a trip to Manchester without visiting the city's fabulous curry houses! For Jason, the 'Curry Cottage' is top.

Howard is rather sensible and notes that it's worth checking out local history. "Perhaps the old canal network and the cotton mills," he suggests. "I would prefer to stray slightly out of the town into the country."

The lads don't swan around in limos when they're in Manchester; it's their home and they behave just as they did before they were famous, going shopping and using public transport, just like everyone else. "I'm always going on the train," says Robbie. "Whenever I come into Manchester to meet the lads, I always get the train back to Stoke."

Media attention was focused on Manchester a few years ago due to the impact made on the charts by the *Happy Mondays* and the *Stone Roses*. *Take That* hope that they are making their own unique contribution in placing Manchester on the musical map. Jason says, "There is no more talent in Manchester than in any other city. I think because the *Stone Roses* and *Happy Mondays* found success, then the media's attention became focused on Manchester."

Mark adds, "I think the Indie scene a few years ago gave Manchester a good name for music, but I'm sure there is probably really no more talent there than anywhere else in the country. But Manchester does have a good atmosphere at the moment, with the football, the music and the sweet shops!"

But more than anything else, Manchester will also be special to *Take That* because it's their home. "Manchester may not be everyone's idea of paradise," says Gary, "but when you're on the road like we are, it can feel that way."

HOWARD

■ **Full name**
Howard Paul Donald

■ **Date of birth**
28th April 1968

■ **Height**
6' 1"

■ **What was your earliest ambition?**
To be an airline pilot.

■ **What was your first record?**
'Ant Music' *Adam and the Ants.*

■ **What was your first musical performance?**
At infant school, singing 'Crazy Horses' by *The Osmonds.*

■ **Who has had the biggest influence on your career?**
I think a mixture of advice from friends and family.

■ **What's the best advice you've ever been given?**
"Do what makes you feel happy." I told myself that.

■ **If there were to be a film made of *The Take That Story*, who would you like to play you?**
Maybe Tom Cruise, because I like the guy and he's a top actor.

■ **What characteristics have you inherited from your parents?**
My parents have a good ear for music. Maybe that's where I get mine from.

■ **What is your best/worst attribute?**
Best - Making up dance routines with Jason, arranging harmonies in songs.
Worst - I don't think I say enough in interviews.

■ **If you hadn't been successful in music, what would you be doing now?**
Probably dancing somewhere very hot.

■ **What is your most treasured possession?**
My family.

■ **Are you superstitious?**
About some things.

■ **What music is on your stereo at the moment?**
Some demos I've recorded myself.

■ **What is your favourite holiday destination and why?**
Anywhere with sun or snow, and peace and quiet.

■ **What are your favourite films?**
Platoon, Philadelphia, Born On The 4th Of July.

■ **Was there ever a moment when you wished you could disappear?**
I once got caught graffiti-ing a bus. I wish I could have disappeared then!

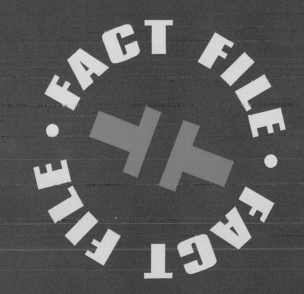

FACT FILE · FACT FILE · FACT FILE

DONALD

"We all have the determination to reach our dreams" Mark

Looking at Mark Owen's boyish face, it's hard to imagine him with a greased quiff and curled lip Elvis Presley style! But it was actually the late, great vocalist who first set Mark on the road to stardom.

Mark's mum, Mary, was a big Elvis fan and as children, Mark and his sister shared her adoration. "We were both mad on Elvis Presley," he remembers. "We used to brush our hair back, put on blue suede shoes and tight trousers and mimic the King to mum's Elvis records. I was hooked on performing from then on!"

But music wasn't Mark's only passion when he was growing up. Although he appeared in a number of school plays, he was also very interested in sport and especially football. His skills, usually on the midfield, won him a large collection of trophies and at the age of twelve, he decided he wanted to become a professional player. He was disappointed at being turned down after trials with Manchester United and Huddersfield Town, but Rochdale were more encouraging. "They did actually say I could come up whenever I wanted," he recalls, "but I never bothered going back up again. It was too much like hard work and made me realise I wouldn't be a footballer after all!" Nevertheless, although he didn't succeed professionally, Mark remains a big football fan, which has led to him being nicknamed 'Booter' by the rest of the band, because he plays whenever he has the chance!

Abandoning his dreams of becoming a football star, Mark left school and found a job working in an Oldham boutique called Zuttis, which, as a fervent follower of fashion, he enjoyed greatly. In fact, he still goes back to visit the store and staff when he has some time off in Manchester! He then went on to work in a branch of Barclays Bank in Oldham, but his career as a banker only lasted two months due to a fateful meeting that was to change the course of his life...

Mark still had an abiding love of music and he pestered a friend of his sister Tracey, a keyboard player in a band, to take him down to Manchester's Strawberry Studios. He began helping out, doing odd jobs and making tea, and it was while he was hanging out at the studio that he met Gary. He started to go round to Gary's house to watch him make demo tapes and one day, Gaz asked him if he'd like to sing backing vocals. They ended up forming a duo called *The Cutest Rush*, which was to become two fifths of *Take That.*

Now Mark is well on the way to emulating the success of his hero Elvis. But he knows only too well, from Presley's tragic example, the pitfalls that can beset a world famous artist and Mark's feet remain firmly rooted on the ground. "I think one of the reasons we've done so well is because of the way we are - five quite normal lads," he says. "I feel a lot of people are looking for us to change and I only hope that we won't."

Take That in the studio

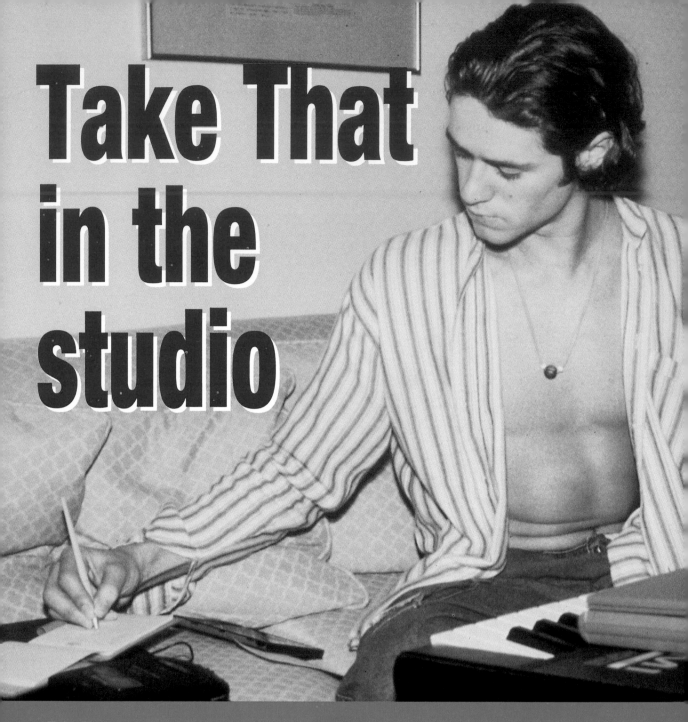

Take That are master craftsmen when it comes to the art of making classic pop records. But how do they go about recording each new hit?

According to Mark, the atmosphere in the studio is usually pretty easy-going. "It's a bit of a sit down, eat lots of food, play cards and wait 'til you're called type thing when we're in the studio," he says. "There is no person really in charge. It's all quiet and relaxed."

"It's definitely a democratic process," agrees Howard, "which involves vocals, where to record it, which products to use or are we going to have beans on toast for tea at the studio!"

"It's democratic, yes," Gary jokes. "I'm in charge!"

It's true that Gary writes songs in his own studio at home and generally presents them to the band in demo form before the band enter the studio. But it doesn't end there. The others suggest arrangements and backing vocals, shaping the song into a recognisable *Take That* hit.

When it comes to deciding which cover versions to record however, the band turn to some very influential outside voices - their mums! Apparently, they are frequently consulted when *Take That* are looking for older material to cover. "We bring them in, because they know all the old records!" Jason says.

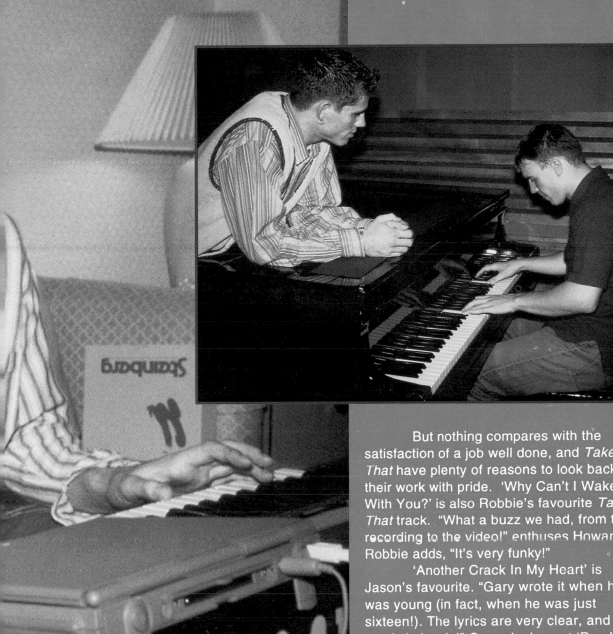

But nothing compares with the satisfaction of a job well done, and *Take That* have plenty of reasons to look back on their work with pride. 'Why Can't I Wake Up With You?' is also Robbie's favourite *Take That* track. "What a buzz we had, from the recording to the video!" enthuses Howard. Robbie adds, "It's very funky!"

'Another Crack In My Heart' is Jason's favourite. "Gary wrote it when he was young (in fact, when he was just sixteen!). The lyrics are very clear, and the music is lovely!" Gary singles out 'Pray', "I love the lyrics." Mark can't decide which *Take That* song he likes best! "I love 'Why Can't I Wake Up With You?', 'Pray', 'Love Ain't Here' and 'Babe', because I think those type of songs get the most out of us vocally."

Take That are all great fans of the classic singer-songwriters like George Michael, Elton John, Neil Young and Bruce Springsteen. "My favourite songwriter is probably Prince for songs like 'Purple Rain' and 'Nothing Compares 2 U'," says Mark.

Most of all, Mark says he'd look up to "anybody who tries damn hard to get better! I really admire Gary for his talent, Jason for his commitment, Howard for his musical ear (he used to have two, but one fell off!!) and Rob for his voice - and our manager Nigel for putting up with five monkeys!"

Although the basics of *Take That*'s songs are moulded outside the studio, there's a lot of hard work to be done once in the recording studio. Recording 'Relight My Fire' was fraught with problems. Originally, Robbie was going to take the lead, and Howard the backing vocals. But it just didn't sound right until Gary and Lulu took their respective places, giving the band their second No.1 single.

Howard names 'Why Can't I Wake Up With You?' as the most difficult single to record, "The vocals are complex and we recorded it into the early hours of the morning - 4am!" Yet it is his favourite single to date.

"I never imagined that I would be famous" Jason

They say that twins share a special relationship, and that's certainly true of Jason Orange and his brother Justin, who was born twenty minutes after him. Mum Jennifer says that as children Jason and Justin appeared to communicate in their own private language, and always stuck up for each other. In fact, they are so close that when they were at school, Jason was once punished for something that Justin did - without telling on him! "If one was off ill, the other would go sick too, so the ill one wouldn't be left on his own," adds Jason. But then, the Orange family, Mum and her six sons - Jason, Justin, Simon, Dominic, Samuel and Oliver - have always been very close.

Jason was brought up as a Mormon, which involves certain dietary restrictions, and he still drinks mineral water or vegetable juice in preference to tea and coffee. In fact, Jay takes a very health conscious approach to food in general. He is a vegetarian - but has been known to cheat with portions of fish and chicken!

At school, Jason excelled at sports, especially football, running and swimming, but he was a shy child and like Howard, often played truant. He gained an apprenticeship in decorating when he left school, which he quite enjoyed at the time, but now admits, "When the band started gaining my interest more and more, I just knew I didn't want to spend the rest of my life working there. I wanted to get out."

His escape to stardom began with a fateful meeting with Howard Donald at a Manchester club called the Apollo. At the time, they were both members of rival breakdance troupes - Jason's was *Street Machine*, while Howard was in the *RDS Royals* - but their mutual enthusiasm for dancing forged their friendship and

they started to create routines together. They decided to form their own troupe called *Street Beat* and approached Nigel Martin Smith to manage them. He recognised the talent they could bring to a new band he was forming and introduced them to Gary and Mark.

Jason recalls the first time *Take That* started to work together. "I was young and hopeful," he says. "I met four other guys who had the same hope. We knew as soon as we met each other

that we had something. There was just a certain vibe in the room. I was unaware of the lads' talents until we really started to get down to business."

He still can't quite believe how successful *Take That* have been. "I never dreamed we'd be where we are now. It's incredible!" he gasps. But Jason is well aware of the fickle nature of fame. "I only have one ambition in life," he says, "and that is to be happy. A cliche, I know, but true."

GARY BARLOW

FACT FILE

- **Full name**
Gary Barlow

- **Date of birth**
20th January 1971

- **Height**
5' 9"

- **What was your earliest ambition?**
To be a spaceman.

- **What was your first record?**
'Living Next Door To Alice' by Smokey.

- **What was your first musical performance?**
At a labour club in North Wales when I was eleven.

- **Who has had the biggest influence on your career?**
Elton John and all the boys from *Take That* and my manager.

- **What's the best advice you've ever been given?**
Don't eat yellow snow!

- **If there were to be a film made of *The Take That Story*, who would you like to play you?**
Whoopi Goldberg.

- **What characteristics have you inherited from your parents?**
Being good with money and having a realistic outlook on life.

- **What is your best/worst attribute?**
My voice is the best, my dancing is the worst.

- **If you hadn't been successful in music, what would you be doing now?**
Playing piano in a restaurant.

- **What is your most treasured possession?**
The chain around my neck.

- **Are you superstitious?**
Yes, I always say a prayer before going on stage.

- **What music is on your stereo at the moment?**
Aaron Neville.

- **What is your favourite holiday destination and why?**
Home is the best holiday ever.

- **What is your favourite film?**
Philadelphia.

- **Was there ever a moment when you wished you could disappear?**
Only after watching *The Invisible Man* when I was young.

Take That

on Tour

The band are unanimous - the best part of being in *Take That* is performing live. "It is not glamorous on tour, and it is hard work, but we do have a great laugh," says Howard.

At least these days, the band has reached a level of success where they can travel in the comparative comfort of a tour bus, stay in nice hotels and play in venues with decent facilities. It wasn't always so! "In our early days, we had to perform on some very small stages," recalls Jason, "And once or twice I would fall off! But I would like to play a club gig again, just as a one-off to remind me of the old days; maybe Ritzy's in Leeds."

These days, instead of driving up and down the motorways of Britain, *Take That* are visiting places they never thought they'd see. Gary was knocked out by Japan, "The food is ace and the place is so cool!" while Howard has fallen in love with New York. "It is a really happening

place," he says. "It's so exciting."

But days on the road can be quite monotonous. Travelling from town to town in their tour bus, the band try to stave off boredom by reading, playing computer games, strumming guitars and watching videos. And with the boys' irrepressible sense of humour, things are never dull for long. Howard generally has his camcorder at the ready to capture the tour's more light-hearted moments.

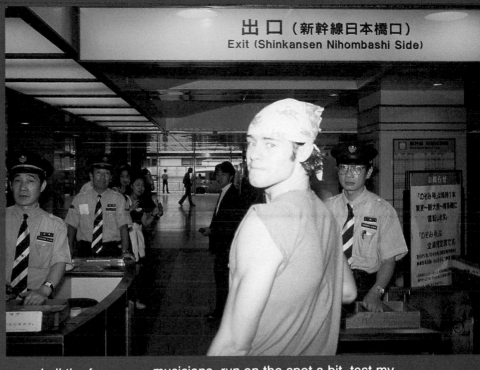

出口（新幹線日本橋口）
Exit (Shinkansen Nihombashi Side)

"Our bus broke down once and all the fans following had to give us a lift!" laughs Gary.

And then, there are the jokes they like to play on each other. According to Jason, Gary has the most annoying habit - "he flicks my ears all the time!"

More amusing is a wind-up the other band members once carried out on Robbie. "We once told Robbie that a magazine was going to take pictures of him nude for £10,000!" chuckles Mark. "Every night for a week, he kept asking us whether we thought his willy was big enough!"

As evening approaches, *Take That* prepare for that night's performance. Jason says he warms up for about 15 minutes. Mark too, "An hour before the show, I get a shower, do some stretches, do some vocals...hug everybody in sight, do more stretches, more vocals and totally tire myself out before I even get on stage!" And in those few moments before facing the audience? "I hug and kiss all the band and all the

musicians, run on the spot a bit, test my microphone and earphones, say a little prayer to myself and listen to the crowd to get the atmosphere."

All too quickly, the show is over and *Take That* take time to reflect. "Being on stage is by far the best part of touring," says Mark. "Seeing the delight on the audience's faces and coming off stage knowing you've done your best - then laughing if one of the lads or yourself has made a mistake!"

"The whole touring life is mega," Jason sums up. "We have a great family vibe. There is no greater feeling than being stood behind the curtain before it drops to reveal a very large, loud, excited crowd, who have all come to see you!"

"I really didn't think we could ever be a band" Robbie

It's very easy to see how Robbie Williams has been influenced by his parents. His mother used to be a singer and his father was comedian Pete Conway, who reached the finals of *New Faces* in 1974. Their talents are reflected both in Robbie's strong vocal ability and in his reputation for being 'the joker' in *Take That*.

On 13th February, 1974 when Robbie was born, his parents were running The Red Lion pub, next to Port Vale football ground - a fact that was to trigger off his life-long devotion to the football team. At the age of three, Robbie moved to Stoke with his mum and sister Sally. Robbie's mum has always been supportive of her son's showbiz career.

Although Robbie had no formal acting training, he became involved with Stoke on Trent's Theatre, taking part in productions like *Pickwick, Fiddler On The Roof* and *Oliver!,* and also acquired a minor role in the long-running tv soap, *Brookside*.

When he left school at sixteen, Robbie wanted to be an actor, but he went into double-glazing sales instead and found it "utterly soul destroying". In fact, Robbie is so honest that he couldn't help telling would-be customers that the windows were rubbish - so it's not surprising he didn't make many sales!

When Gary, Mark, Jason and Howard placed an ad in a local newspaper for a fifth member for the new band they were forming, Robbie's mum encouraged him to apply. Consequently he was asked to come to Nigel Martin Smith's office for an audition. He sang them a song from *Joseph And The Amazing Technicolor Dreamcoat*, but now admits, "I remember thinking what a weird bunch of lads they were, and I really didn't think we could ever be a band." The other band members however, were more favourably impressed with Robbie. "I remember him being very funny and very confident," recalls Mark.

Three or four weeks later, Robbie received the call offering him a place in *Take That*. "I was over the moon," he says. "By this time, I did actually think that they were going to be successful."

However, it wasn't all smooth sailing to start off with. Robbie remembers the band's early rehearsals with some embarrassment. "I was terrible," he says. "I didn't dance well and kept getting everything wrong. The others were excellent, but I slowly got the hang of it and caught up with them."

■ **Full name**
Jason Thomas Orange

■ **Date of birth**
10th July 1970

■ **Height**
6' 0"

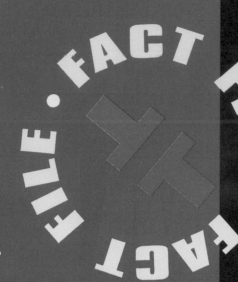

■ **What was your earliest ambition?**
To dance on stage behind somebody famous. I never imagined that I would be famous.

■ **What was your first record?**
'The Wall' *Pink Floyd*.

■ **What was your first musical performance?**
I never performed musically on stage until I was with *Take That*.

■ **Who has had the biggest influence on your career?**
My friends and family. The people I grew up with always encouraged me to do well.

■ **What's the best advice you've ever been given?**

Live each moment of your life like it is an unrepeatable miracle - because that's what it is.

■ **If there were to be a film made of *The Take That Story*, who would you like to play you?**
Definitely Tom Cruise. He is a great actor.

JASON ORANGE

■ What characteristics have you inherited from your parents?
My father's generosity and my mother's strength, sensitivity, determination, kindness and smile.

■ What is your best/worst attribute?
Best - I think I'm quite kind. Worst - I get upset and my moods are sometimes out of my control.

■ If you hadn't been successful in music, what would you be doing now?
I was always hoping to see the world, so maybe I would be in a job that allowed me to travel. Or maybe I wouldn't have a job, maybe I would just travel.

■ What is your most treasured possession?
My family - but I don't really possess them do I? So I will say my bookcase.

■ Are you superstitious?
No.

■ What music is on your stereo at the moment?
'Unplugged' Eric Clapton.

■ What is your favourite holiday destination and why?
Anywhere by the sea. Mauritius was lovely. I was alone.

■ What is your favourite film?
Awakenings.

■ Was there ever a moment when you wished you could disappear?
No!

29

Take That Too

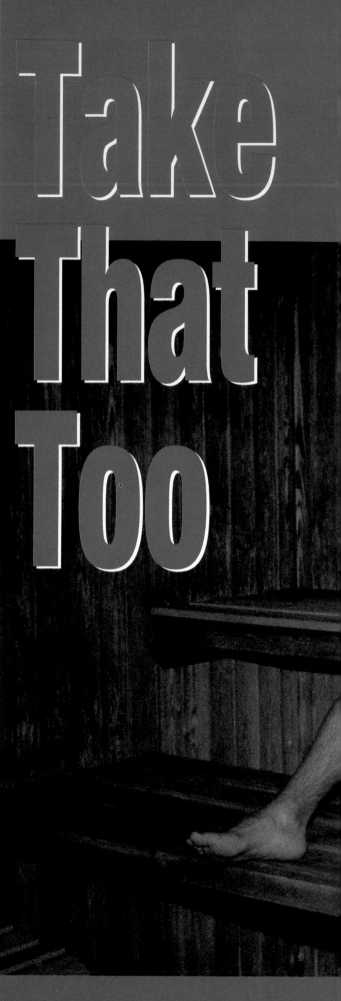

With making records and touring the world, *Take That* don't get much time for relaxation. But when they do, they're not likely to be seen in trendy clubs or jetting off on expensive holidays. They prefer to go home and savour the simpler pleasures of life - the things that most people outside *Take That*'s hectic world take for granted.

"I guess going on holiday is the best way for us to take time out," says Mark, "but at the moment, if we get a few days off, you really want to spend it at home with your family and friends."

When asked what he likes to do in his spare time, Robbie replies, "Rollerblading, or drinking Lowenbrau down the pub, then combining the two!", while Gary reckons he can get away from it all simply by taking a hot bath!

Thousands of girls would undoubtedly like to share Jason's fantasy of a relaxing evening: "To sit at home, rocking on my rocking chair with a glass of wine, mellow music and a little bit of intimacy with someone I care about. If the situation becomes more intimate though, the rocking chair becomes inappropriate...!"

Sport is a favourite method of relaxation for every member of *Take That*. Robbie loves to watch his beloved Port Vale, while Mark likes to kick a ball around himself and boxing is Howard's favourite sport. In fact, Howie once sat up all night with Mark and Robbie to watch the Bruno v. Lewis match - despite having to record a tv show at 7 that morning!

Take That are also always happy to combine their work with play to raise funds for a worthwhile cause. They've lent their support to a number of different charities over the years, but one of the most enjoyable charitable activities they've undertaken was a show to raise funds for the Bryan Robson Scanner Appeal, when they ended up having a kick-about with the Manchester United Football Team on the turf of Old Trafford.

"I'm happy that we have done things for all sorts of charities," says Mark, "and I'll be glad to carry on doing that in the future. I do hate to see homelessness though, it saddens me."

"There are so many sad things in life, but I think Aids saddens me the most," says Howard. "It's so cruel. In this material world, people should be allowed to have sex or make love to anybody they would like to, providing it's the right age of consent. But now we all have to be so careful."

Fame can be of great assistance when it comes to raising money for charity - but what about when you want to have a relaxing day off? How do *Take That* cope with the fact that they're recognised wherever they go?

"Fame is something you have to get used to and believe me, I'm still not used to it," says Howard. "Although it is very nice to live with, I would like to keep my private life."

Jason believes that *is* possible. "The biggest myth about fame is that you loose your private life. Although you have to make a few sacrifices and be a bit cagey about your business, you don't lose your private life."

"I think I cope with fame pretty well," says Mark. "I don't lock myself in my room. I like to get out and do things - go shopping, see my friends, go to the pub. To be honest, when you're doing what we do, you can sometimes forget that you're so-called 'famous' and you think to yourself, 'Why is everybody looking at me?'"

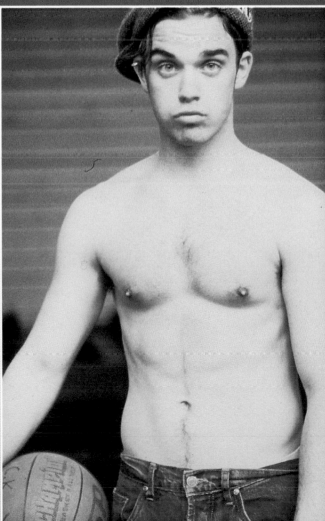

■ Full name
Mark Anthony Owen

■ Date of birth
24th January 1972

■ Height
5' 7"

■ What was your earliest
ambition?
For as long as I can remember,
I always wanted to fly. When I
realised that might be a bit
difficult, I took to being able to
swim and breathe under water.
After nearly drowning myself in
the bath, I bought a football
and started to practise with that
for a laugh - and I had most
success there!

■ What was your first record?
The theme to *E.T.* The cover
was a moon, with E.T. flying on
a BMX with the lad riding it.

■ What was your first musical
performance?
Me and my sister Tracey used
to do rock and roll shows in
front of the house with a tape
recorder. I used to grease my
hair and my mum would kill
me, because it wouldn't wash
out for days!

■ Who has had the biggest
influence on your career?
I think all my family and friends
have really helped me, but the
desire to be like, and as good
as, the other lads keeps me
going.

■ What's the best advice
you've ever been given?
Believe in yourself and no
matter what's happening, just
smile and act relaxed.

■ If there were to be a film
made of *The Take That Story*,
who would you like to play
you?
It would have been nice for
somebody like River Phoenix
to play me, because I thought
he was a great actor, but with
me being small, maybe
Macauley Culkin would be a
better idea!

■ What characteristics have
you inherited from your
parents?
I worry a lot like my mum and I
laugh at my own jokes, like my
dad.

■ What is your best/worst
attribute?
My best attribute is probably
that I care a lot about the
presentation and image of the
band. My worst is that I care
too much about it.

■ If you hadn't been
successful in music, what
would you be doing now?
I would probably be at college
and still be trying to make it as
a pro footballer.

■ What is your most treasured
possession?
My lizard is my most treasured
possession and my first car, a
white Ford Fiesta. Although
the car keeps breaking down, I
still really love it.

■ Are you superstitious?
Yes, I don't walk under ladders
and that, so I suppose I am.

■ What music is on your
stereo at the moment?
The new *Color Me Badd*
album, and *U2* keeps finding its
way in there.

■ What is your favourite
holiday destination and why?
My best holiday to date has
been to Kavos, Corfu with my
mates when I was eighteen.

■ What is your favourite film?
I really enjoyed *Philadelphia*,
which is the last film I watched,
but *Can't Buy Me Love* and
The Outsiders are two of my
all-time favourites.

■ Was there ever a moment
when you wished you could
disappear?
I do get embarrassed quite
easily. I remember singing and
dancing in my bedroom once
and when I went to the window,
there were fans outside and
they were all laughing at me! I
felt very embarrassed!

MARK

OWEN

FACT FILE · FACT FILE · FACT FILE · FACT FILE ·

"I don't ever want to change" Howard

It was always obvious that Howard Donald would find a career in show business. It's in his blood! His mother Kathleen was a singer, while his father Keith used to teach Latin American dancing, and the talents of both are combined in their son.

Young Howard was not too interested in studying, finding his BMX bike and breakdancing way more attractive than books. At school, he played the classroom clown and more than once skipped classes. In fact, he once stayed away for five whole weeks - and his mother never found out until he told her recently!

When he left school, Howard took a job as a vehicle restorer at a garage. But his interest in breakdancing continued and he became a member of a breakdancing troupe called the *RDS Royals*. No mean dancer himself - (he actually secured a solo spot on Pete Waterman's *Hitman And Her* tv show) - he was knocked out by Jason's skills when he saw him dancing in local clubs. "I used to watch him dance and think, 'God, I wish I could breakdance like him'," he says. "We got talking and got on really well."

The pair formed the troupe *Street Beat* and, through Nigel Martin Smith, were introduced to the other prospective members of *Take That*. "It was weird," he comments, "I already knew Jason, so it was good that I knew somebody when we met with the rest, but we all got on so well."

Within the band, Howard, along with Jason, is *Take That's* main choreographer - and he's all round a very physical guy! In fact, the rest of the band have nicknamed him 'The Body' (which he hates!), because he works out at every available opportunity.

But Howard is also blossoming as a musican. He arranges the harmonies in *Take That's* songs and is working hard at his songwriting. He takes a keyboard on tour, so he can practise and write in his hotel room, and Howard has spent much of his wages on constructing a studio at home. "It's only half built, but I've only been doing it for two years," he says.

Finally, all the hard work is paying off for Howard, with the inclusion of 'If This Is Love', (a song he co-wrote with producer David James), on *Take That's* album, 'Everything Changes'. Howard modestly credits Gary for providing him with the inspiration to pen his own material. "I'm proud of Gary and all the songs he's written," he comments. "But I'm also proud of myself for writing a song and I think Gary's proud of me!"

Despite his increased profile within the band, Howard is adamant that fame will not affect him. "I think a lot of people like to imagine fame has changed me," he says, "but personally, I don't think I've changed in the way I act. I'm still as down to earth as I ever was and I don't ever want to change."

Memorable

Moments

1. The First Meeting

If band manager Nigel Martin Smith hadn't had the foresight to introduce breakdance team *Street Beat* to vocal duo *The Cutest Rush*, *Take That* might never have existed! The four hit it off from the start and decided to advertise for a fifth band member. Robbie Williams answered the ad and the rest is history...

2. First Top 10 Single

"I remember we were all sitting down together at our manager's house, wondering if it would ever happen to us," says Robbie. "Then 'It Only Takes A Minute' came out and that was it really." After previous chart disappointments, 'It Only Takes A Minute' peaked at No.7 in May 1992, proving to the pop world that *Take That* really were a force to be reckoned with!

3. Release Of First Album

'Take That And Party' was released in August 1992 and was a phenomenally successful debut, selling almost 700,000 copies in the U.K. alone and achieving double platinum status. "There was a time when we'd have been happy with a silver disc," says Robbie. "We still would. But to get a double platinum is beyond all our wildest dreams."

4. First Major U.K. Tour

With their popularity rising fast, *Take That* undertook their first major U.K. tour in November of 1992. "We honestly didn't know if anyone would come," confesses Gary. "I remember we kept asking our tour promoter if he thought we'd sell any tickets!"

5. First No.1 Single

In July 1993, *Take That* became only the 23rd artist in chart history to go straight into the singles chart at No.1. Howard remembers receiving the news. "I was at home with my

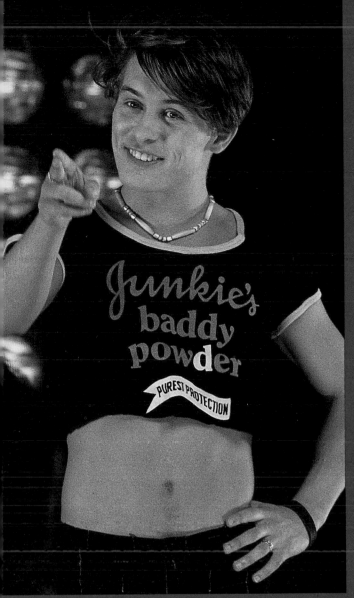

7. 'Relight My Fire' Goes To No.1
Another *Take That* song entered the chart at No.1 in September 1993 and *Take That* become only the second act to achieve this with two consecutive singles, (the other artist being *Slade*, more than twenty years ago!). The track was a cover of a Dan Hartman disco classic and Lulu guested on backing vocals.

8. The Release Of 'Everything Changes'
Take That's second album went straight into the charts at No.1 and platinum within its first week of release. The record features Mark's lead vocal debut with 'Babe' and Howard's first recorded song, 'If This Is Love', co-written with producer David James.

9. Third No.1 Single
Mark's memorable performances of 'Babe' during *Take That*'s autumn tour, meant little

family, it was a very emotional moment." The release was 'Pray' and it stayed in the top slot for four weeks selling more than half a million copies. "I probably didn't act the way people would expect someone who had just got their first No.1 to act," says Jason. "I found it quite hard to acknowledge." Mark had no such problem! "We had to leave our families to go to Wales to rehearse. Me and Howard were getting drunk, celebrating in the back of the car!"

6. First Arena Tour
Take That played their first arena tour over seven dates from 20th to 26th July 1993. By this time, their success was such that all the shows sold out well in advance. "It's important to show people that we are a performing band," Gary said at the time. "That's what we do best; we go out and we sing and we dance."

surprise at their third consecutive No.1 single. Many thought it would be 1993's Christmas No.1, but it was pipped to the post by Mr Blobby!

10. First Full European Tour
Spring 1994, and *Take That* mania spread across Europe as the band undertook their first full European tour. Mark says he was surprised at how well the whole tour went. "It was all a bit new to us and the fans, but they were great."

Gary still names England as his favourite touring country and the feeling is unanimous. "Nothing beats the English crowd," sums up Jason.

"Great Britain has surprised us," says Howard. "The devotion and longevity of support and I really hope we can please everyone for years to come."

ROBBIE WILLIAMS

■ **Full name**
Robert Peter Williams

■ **Date of birth**
13th February 1974

■ **Height**
6' 2"

■ **What was your earliest ambition?**
To be famous.

■ **What was your first record?**
'Hello John Got A New Motor' by Alexi Sayle.

■ **What was your first musical performance?**
Guitar tech for *The Stones*, 'Urban Jungle Tour' 1988/89. I replaced Ronnie Wood's guitar string on stage!

■ **Who has had the biggest influence on your career?**
Mike Stevens, Musical Director of our band.

■ **What's the best advice you've ever been given?**
Run!

■ **If there were to be a film made of *The Take That Story*, who would you like to play you?**
One of the McGann brothers.

■ **What characteristics have you inherited from your parents?**
Plastic teeth, feet and aluminium tonsils!

■ **What is your best/worst attribute?**
I am a bit lazy.

■ **If you hadn't been successful in music, what would you be doing now?**
An out-of-work actor.

■ **What is your most treasured possession?**
My family.

■ **Are you superstitious?**
Very.

■ **What music is on your stereo at the moment?**
The Beatles.

■ **What is your favourite holiday destination and why?**
Miami, it is so laid back.

■ **What is your favourite film?**
Not got one.

■ **Was there ever a moment when you wished you could disappear?**
Yes, when I bet a man £1,000 that I could disappear!

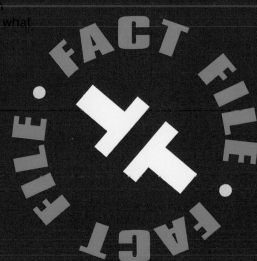

FACT FILE · FACT FILE · FACT FILE ·

41

Disc⊘graphy

Could It Be Magic
December 1992

No. 3

Why Can't I Wake Up With You?
February 1993

No. 2

Pray
July 1993

No. 1

Relight My Fire
September 1993

No. 1

Everything Changes
April 1994

No. 1

SINGLES

Do What You Like
July 1991

No. 82

Promises
November 1991

No. 38

Once You've Tasted Love
January 1992

No. 47

It Only Takes A Minute
May 1992

No. 7

I Found Heaven
August 1992

No. 15

A Million Love Songs
September 1992

No. 7

ALBUMS

Take That And Party
August 1992

No. 2

Everything Changes
October 1993

No. 1

VIDEOS

Take That And Party
December 1992

No. 1

The Party/Live At Wembley
November 1993

No. 1

At the moment, *Take That* are riding on a wave of success, but how do they see their future? "I know we all have the determination to reach all our dreams," says Mark, adding cautiously, "but I suppose we never know what will happen in the future."

That's Ambition

One thing that does appear certain however, is that the solid base of friendship on which the band was formed will continue to last, whatever fate throws at them. When asked what they think they'll be doing in five years time, there is a marked similarity of response.

"It is hard to say, but I hope we are still like family and hopefully still making records," says Howard.

"Hopefully, we will all be together and still touring," agrees Mark, "but even if the band finishes, I will always get together with the other lads."

"I hope we are sat in an Indian restaurant, celebrating our friendship and more No.1s," announces Jason. "In reality, I will probably be married with a few babies, or writing a book on how the business stole my identity and my money!" he adds.

As *Take That's* main songwriter and lead vocalist, it is inevitable that from time to time, rumours will surface that Gary will pursue a solo career. But he delivers a firm commitment to the future of the band when he says, "While I'm in *Take That*, all my ambitions will be for the band."

That's not to rule out little side projects in the future, which needn't threaten the existence of the band. Robbie has a secret desire to work with top producer Quincy Jones, while Mark wouldn't mind doing a duet with Mariah Carey or Annie Lennox.

A natural progression for a number of chart-topping stars has been to move into the world of the cinema and that's something Robbie, Jason and Howard have expressed an interest in. Robbie has long cherished a desire to star in a remake of *The Magnificent Seven*, while Jason would like to play a lead role opposite Steffi Graf, because it would be her first attempt at acting too!

Mark would also like to take a part on the big screen, but he harbours ambitions that are a little nearer home. "I would love to do a film with the other lads," he says, "and I keep asking the record company, 'Can I shoot a video?', but they pretend not to hear and just laugh!"

Who knows what exciting offers could be waiting just around the corner? But for the time being, Gary knows what the immediate future will bring for *Take That*, "Still touring, still recording and still all great friends!"